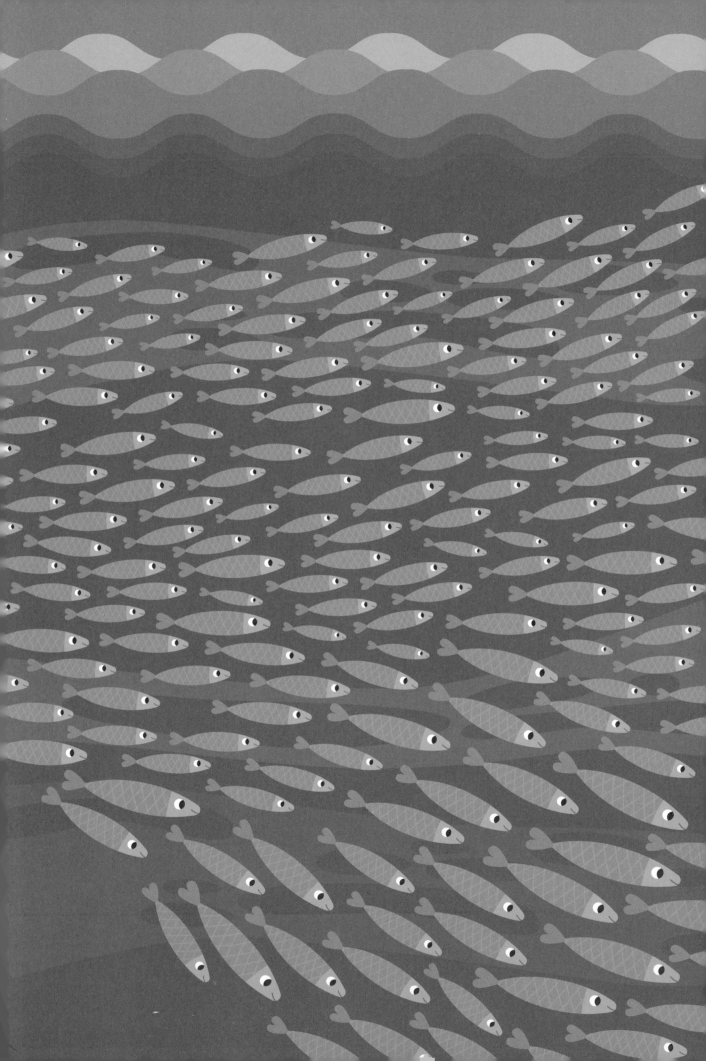

Agnese Baruzzi

Find Me!

Adventures in the Ocean

Play along to
sharpen your vision
and mind

WOLVES AT THE BEACH!

Bernard the wolf could not see very well. But with the help of a friend and a pair of strong glasses, his vision was much better. Now he could spot almost anything in the forest. The other wolves in his pack respected his sharp eyesight.

But the leader of the wolf pack had an
idea that took them all by surprise.

"Let's leave the forest and go to the beach
for a summer vacation!" he said.

"We can have a refreshing swim
whenever we like!

It's so boring eating the same things all the
time: sheep, little pigs, goats, and sometimes
a child if we get lucky.

At the beach, we'll finally be able to
change our diet and

feast on something different, like shrimp
or octopus or tuna.

There will be so much more to sink
our teeth into by the ocean!"

So Bernard was soon at the beach.

He put on his scuba-diving mask and prepared to go into the ocean. But he found out right away that he couldn't see much from behind the cloudy mask!

"Oh no!" Bernard cried.

"I'm just the same short-sighted wolf as ever."

A little red crab happened to be creeping past him.

"Why are you crying, wolf?" she asked.

Bernard explained, "In this scuba mask, I can't see past the end of my tail. I could get lost underwater! And then the other wolves won't think I'm sharp-eyed and fierce anymore."

"Don't worry, wolf!" the little crab told him.

"I'll help you."

"Sharpen your eyes and find me!"

The crab explained, "I'll be hiding in lots of different places so we can explore them together. Everywhere I go, you'll have to find me. We'll see many kinds of fish, jellyfish, octopuses, and whales. Look at them carefully, then answer my questions."

"But beware!" the crab added. "Sometimes in the deep, dark water at the bottom of the ocean, you won't be able to see my red shell. You'll have to look for my shadow instead. Here it is in front of you now."

"By the end of our adventure," the crab declared, "you'll be an eagle-eyed underwater observer!"

"READY, STEADY, GO!"

Who is arguing?

Who is having a snack?

Who has pooped?

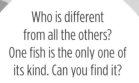

Who is different
from all the others?
One fish is the only one of
its kind. Can you find it?

What might happen to the squid?

What has the ship lost?

Who is wearing eye makeup?

The giant daddy
squid has lost his baby.
Only one of the babies here
is the same as daddy squid.
Can you spot which one?

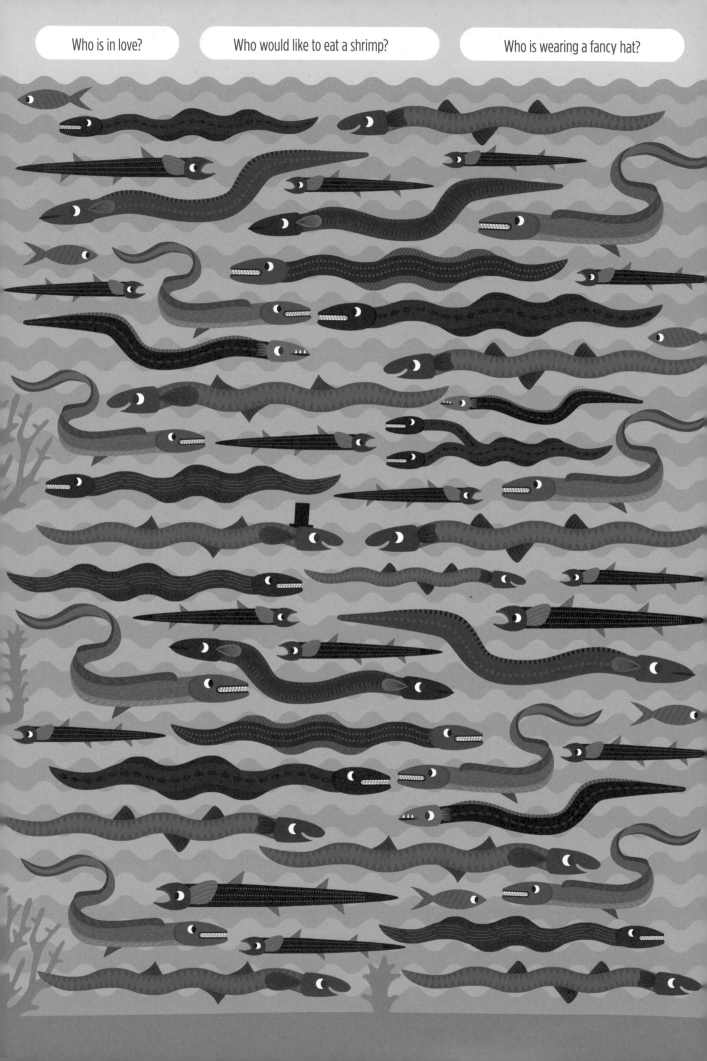

Three mythical beasts
are hiding among the eels.
Where are they?

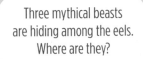

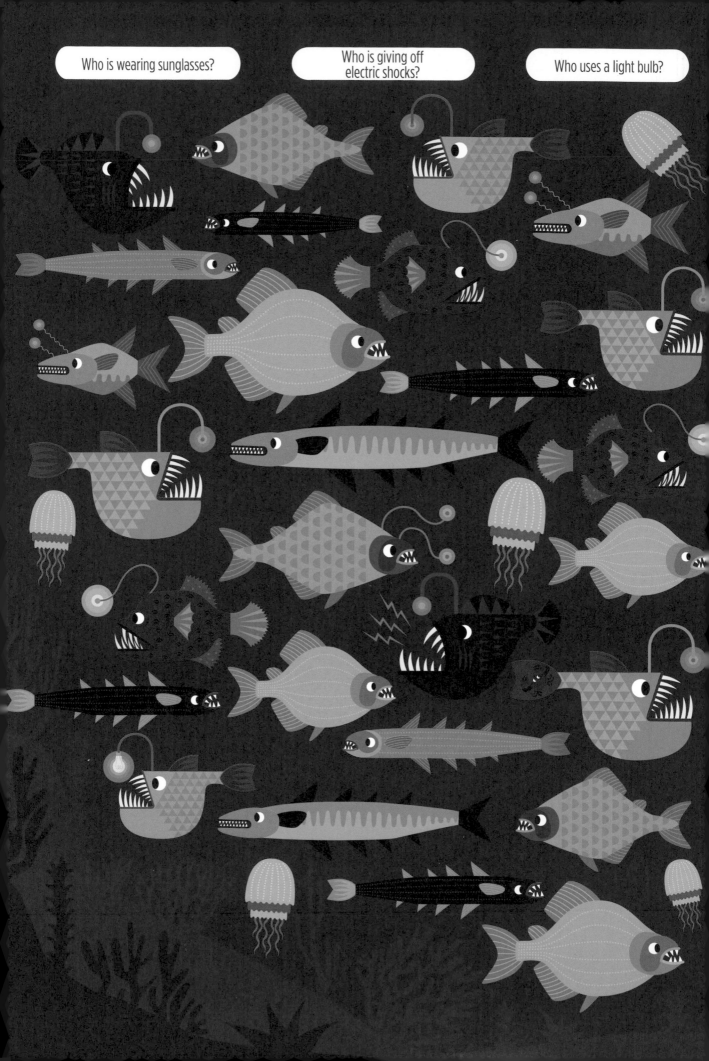

Who is wearing sunglasses?

Who is giving off
electric shocks?

Who uses a light bulb?

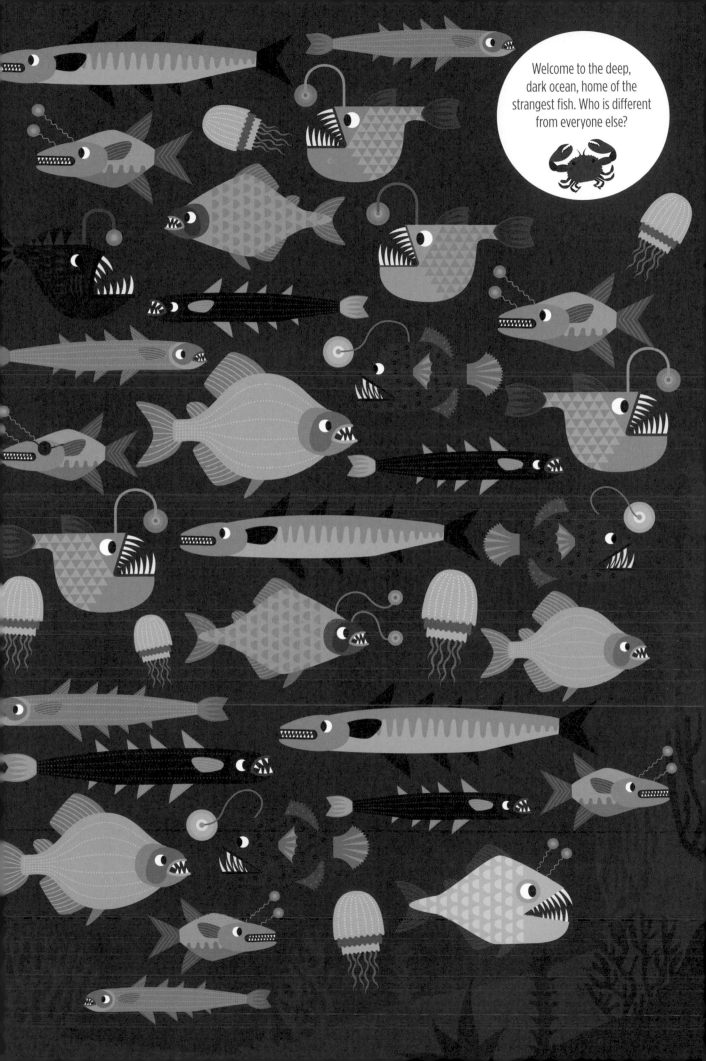

Welcome to the deep, dark ocean, home of the strangest fish. Who is different from everyone else?

Can you find a rolled-up map?

Can you spot a priceless pearl?

Find a fishing hook.

There are lots of shells on the ocean floor. Some are homes to tiny animals. Can you find ten hidden hermit crabs?

Everyone is with their family today, except for three fish that are on their own. Can you spot them?

Find the pairs.
Each shark on the right page
has a twin on the left page.
Can you match them up?

Who has a swimsuit on?

Who is sleeping?

Who has just been born?

Find three starfish.

A pirate has lost his hook. Can you find it?

Can you see a fishbone?

It's easy to get lost on the coral reef. Five mommy fish are sad because they can't find their five little ones. Can you help them?

One mermaid is different from the others.
Which one?

Who is sad?

Who has been stung by a jellyfish?

Find the pairs!
Almost every mermaid
has a twin.

Three objects have fallen into the jellyfish's den, and they don't belong there. Can you find them?

A little boy dropped three things into the ocean. What are they?

Who has lots of spines?

Who is kissing?

Only two fish
look the same.
Can you find them?

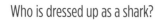

Who is dressed up as a shark?

Who is feeling sad?

Who is yawning?

The sardines are migrating, but three of them are going the wrong way. Can you spot them?

The pirates have lost their treasure! The octopuses stole the three keys to the locks on the chests. Can you find them?

Who does not live in the ocean?

Find three objects lost underwater.

Find my crab family.

Three squid are hiding
among the lobsters.
Try to spot them!

Can you see a jellyfish?

Do you see a turtle?

Can you see an eel?

Did you answer all the questions?

FIND OUT HERE!

You will find the solutions to all the games on the next few pages. Check your powers of observation, and decide if you need to go back and repeat the exercise! You will see that some solutions have:

★ A star to indicate the characters in the main game and in the special questions.

④ Numbers to help you check if you have found all the animal pairs.

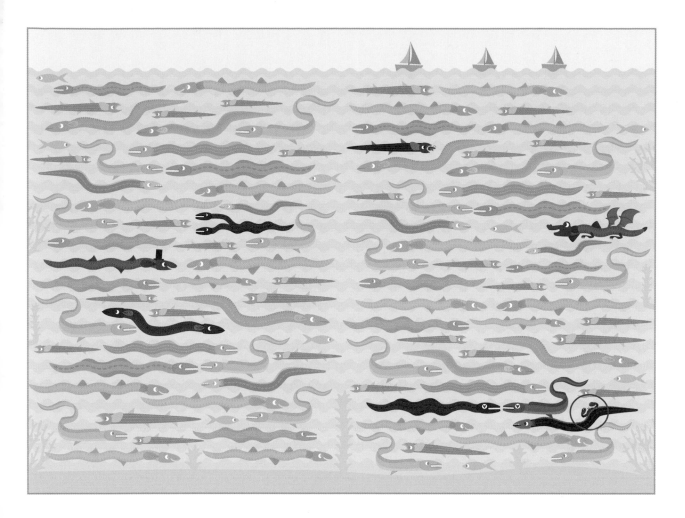

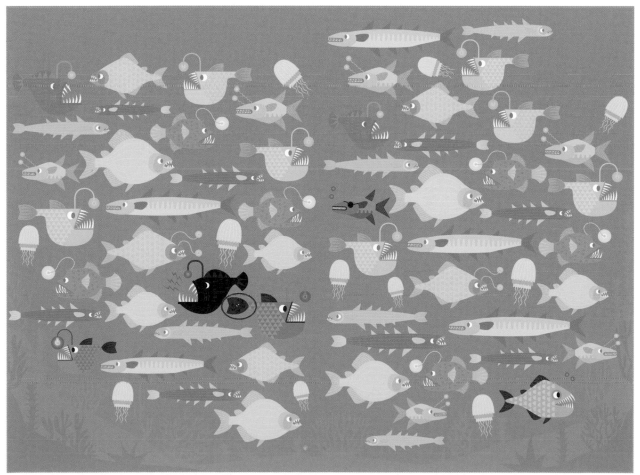

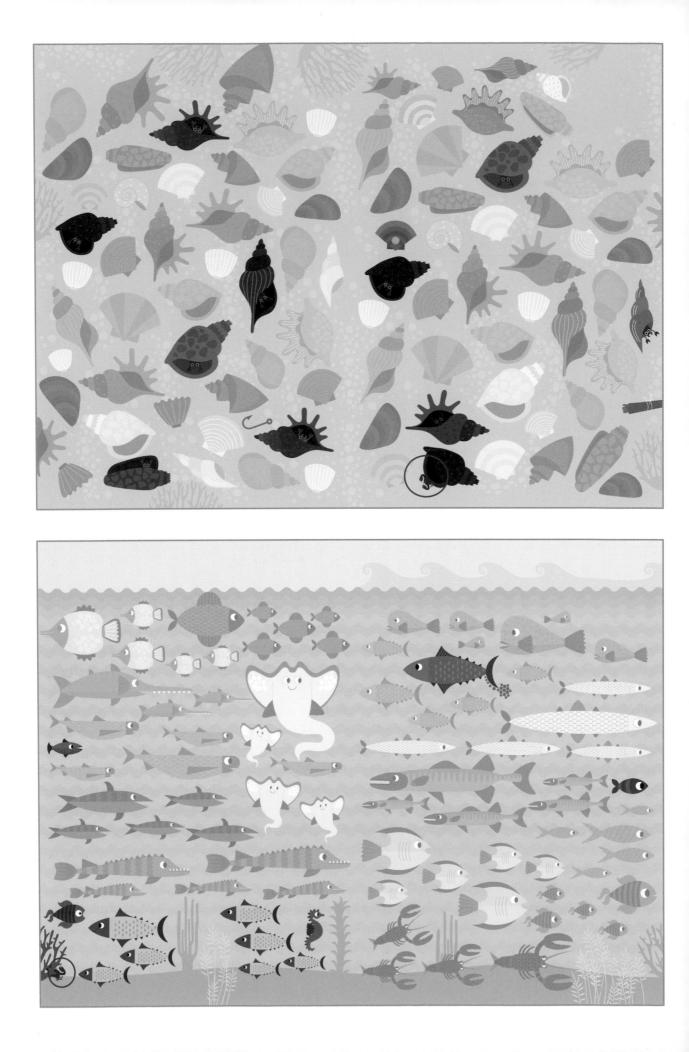

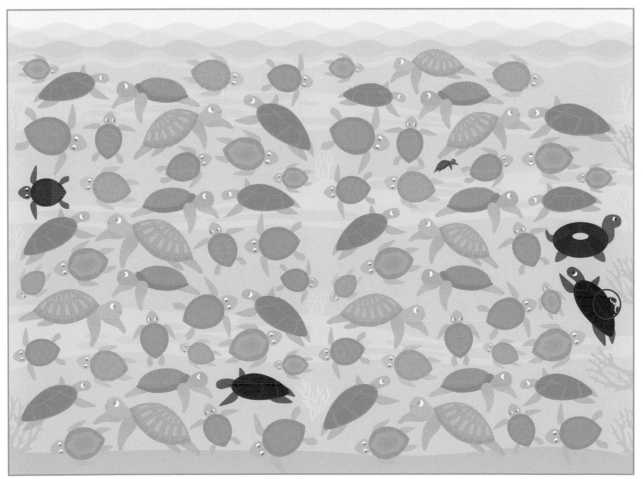

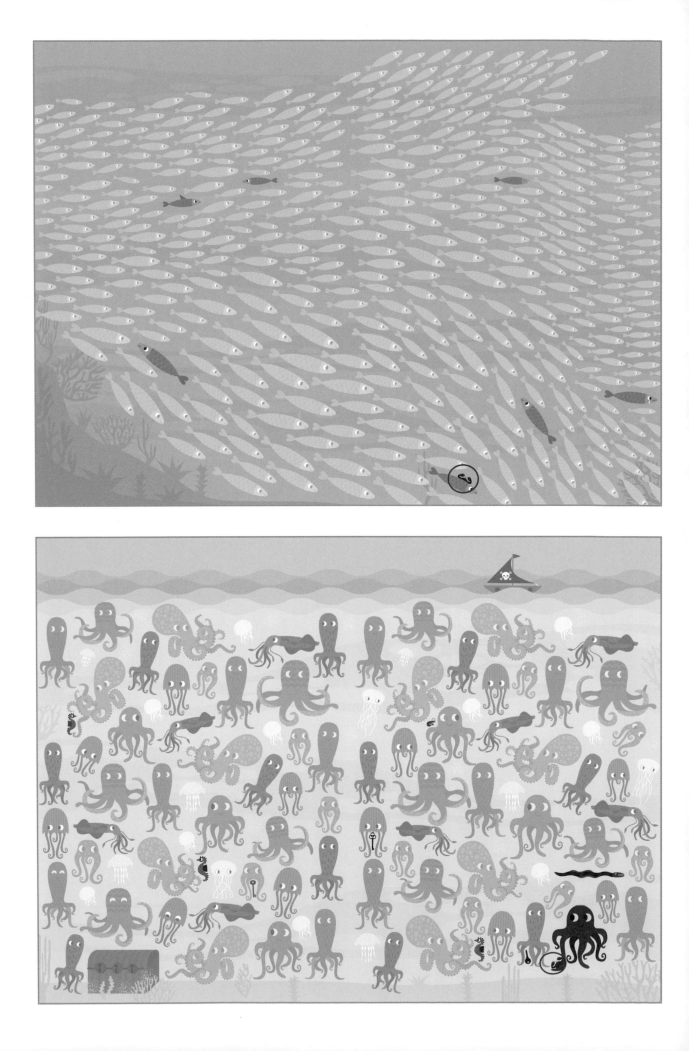

Agnese Baruzzi

Born in 1980, she has a degree in Graphic Design from the High Institute for Artistic Industries (ISIA) in Urbino, Italy. Since 2011, she has been working as an illustrator and author for kids' books in Italy, United Kingdom, Japan, Portugal, United States, France, and Korea. She organizes workshops for kids and adults in schools and libraries, as well as collaborates with agencies, graphic design studios, and publishers. In the last few years Baruzzi has illustrated several books for White Star Kids.

White Star Kids® is a registered trademark property of White Star s.r.l.

© 2019 White Star s.r.l.
Piazzale Luigi Cadorna, 6
20123 Milan, Italy
www.whitestar.it

Translation: Denise Muir

Originally published in 2019 as *Find Me! Ocean Adventures with Bernard the Wolf* by White Star, this North American version titled *Find Me! Adventures in the Ocean* is published in 2020 by Fox Chapel Publishing Company, Inc. Reproduction of its contents is strictly prohibited without written permission from the rights holder.

Happy Fox Books is an imprint of Fox Chapel Publishing Company, Inc., 903 Square Street, Mount Joy, PA 17552.

ISBN 978-1-64124-046-8 (Hardcover)
ISBN 978-1-64124-102-1 (Paperback)

Library of Congress Control Number: 2019955442

To learn more about the other great books from Fox Chapel Publishing, or to find a retailer near you, call toll-free 800-457-9112 or visit us at *www.FoxChapelPublishing.com*.

We are always looking for talented authors. To submit an idea, please send a brief inquiry to acquisitions@foxchapelpublishing.com.

Fox Chapel Publishing makes every effort to use environmentally friendly paper for printing.

Printed in China

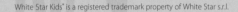